D1349395

VIKINGS
◁ MYTHS AND LEGENDS ▷

Translated by Frances Halton

Illustrations by Marcel Laverdet

Written and edited by Gilles Ragache

CHERRYTREE BOOKS

A Cherrytree Book

Adapted by A S Publishing
from *Les Vikings*
published by Hachette

First published 1992
by Cherrytree Press Ltd
a subsidiary of
The Chivers Company Ltd
Windsor Bridge Road
Bath, Avon BA2 3AX

Reprinted 1993

British Library Cataloguing in Publication Data
Ragache, Gilles
    Vikings.—New ed.—(Myths & Legends
    Series)
    I. Title   II. Halton, Frances
    III. Laverdet, Marcel   IV. Series
    293. 13

    ISBN 0-7451-5166-3

Printed in Hong Kong by Colorcraft Ltd

CONTENTS

▷ GIANTS AND DWARFS ◁

Long before the first humans appeared, the earth was peopled with giants and dwarfs. The very first living being, the giant Ymir, was formed from the ice which covered the world. Soon two more giants appeared, then an enormous cow, Audumla, who gave milk to feed them. Her warm breath and rough tongue melted the ice around her, and a fifth being, Buri, emerged from it.

The first three gods, Odin, Vili and Ve, were descended from Buri and the giants. But a terrible war broke out between gods and giants and Ymir was killed. The gods turned his body into the earth and his blood into the sea; his bones became mountains and his hair forests. Then the gods created plants and animals, and finally the first man and the first woman, whom they made from two tree trunks.

The giants lurked in the far corners of the earth and plotted revenge. From the hearts of volcanoes, the giants of fire caused eruptions and earthquakes. Deep in the oceans, the sea giants unleashed fierce tempests, and the ice giants sent snow and hail from the frozen north. But some giants were friendly. Among these were Mimir, guardian of the fountain of wisdom, who became Odin's friend, and Aegir, a sea giant who was looked on as a god.

Far underground, away from the warring gods and giants, lived the dwarfs. Secretive and timid, they were masters of fire and of metal-work and made weapons with magical properties, so the gods protected them. They made

Odin's spear Gungner, and even created a ship covered in gold which sailed wherever Odin wished, regardless of high seas or headwinds. All the Vikings dreamed of this wonderful ship as they were tossed and battered by the stormy northern seas.

The dwarfs were sometimes malicious and quarrelsome, but they seldom harmed anyone. Although they were not immortal, they could live to an immense age. In the distant mountains of Scandinavia, people still search for their fabulous treasures!

The dwarf smiths were master metalworkers, and made magic weapons for the gods.

The gods were constantly being attacked by giants and monsters. To combat them Odin decided to create a fortified city, called Asgard, where he and the other gods and goddesses could live in safety.

Odin naturally wanted Asgard to be large and splendid. Building it would be an immense task – and one which he and the other gods had no wish to undertake themselves. So they asked a giant who was famous for such works to carry it out for them. The giant agreed to build Asgard, but he asked a high price. The gods must give him the sun, the moon and Freya, the beautiful goddess of love. The gods hesitated when they heard his terms but, after talking them over for a long time, they agreed. However, they imposed conditions which they felt sure that the giant would never be able to fulfil: he must complete the work in less than one year, and without the aid of other giants or even of men. To their surprise, he accepted these conditions without hesitation and the very next day he began work.

In far distant forests, the giant felled the tallest trees and formed them into beams. He shaped huge rocks for his masonry. Asgard took shape so quickly that the gods felt sure the giant was cheating. One night they hid themselves and watched. To their astonishment, they found that the giant's helper was a magic horse, Svadilfari, who carried in the timber and rocks as if they were mere wisps of hay. Then the giant could easily build them up.

Three nights before the deadline – the first day of summer – only the great entrance to the palace was still unfinished. Odin was furious at the thought of losing the sun and the moon, and above all the beautiful goddess Freya. But he had to keep his word.

Then the cunning spirit of fire, Loki, who was a constant companion of the gods, suggested a trick. The gods gave him permission to do anything he liked.

The following night, a spirited mare crossed the path of the giant's horse. Svadilfari had never seen anything so beautiful. He broke his halter and ran off, abandoning his load of stones and timber. He galloped after the irresistible filly. It was three whole days before he returned, by which time it was too late. The last stones were missing from the great entrance when the deadline came.

The giant knew he had been tricked, for although the palace was all but finished, the gods did not have to keep their promise. He flew into a fearful rage, and demanded his full reward, in particular the goddess Freya. Odin refused, and the giant threatened him. Thor, the god of thunder, sprang to his defence and hit the giant a powerful blow with his magic hammer. The giant fell dead.

The gods had won – but by a shabby trick. And they had lost the only person who knew all the secrets of Asgard.

Some time later the mare who had lured away Svadilfari gave birth to a wonderful eight-footed foal. Swifter than lightning, the beast could gallop across the crests of the waves and over the mountain peaks. He was called Sleipnir, and he became the mount of Odin.

Each night the magic stallion Svadilfari carried up the building materials for Asgard.

▷ ODIN THE WISE WARRIOR ◁

Odin was first and foremost the god of war. With his magic spear Gungner in his hand, he threw himself eagerly into the heart of the fiercest battles. To protect himself, he wore a horned helmet covered in gold, a breastplate, and around his waist a belt with a great buckle which when necessary increased his strength tenfold.

In all his battles Odin was accompanied by two giant wolves, and thirteen beautiful warrior maidens known as the Valkyries. They chose the warriors who were to be killed in battle, appearing to them while remaining invisible to everyone else. After the fights, they guided the dead to Valhalla, a paradise specially built for them in Asgard. There they spent their time feasting and telling tales of the glorious battles they had fought.

When Odin was present at their feasts he ate nothing himself, and drank only hydromel, the gods' special drink made from honey. He gave his share of the food to the two great wolves which stood guard on either side of him.

Odin was not just a simple warrior; he was also the god of wisdom, poetry and magic. He had only one eye; he had given the other to the giant Mimir in exchange for a drink from the fountain of wisdom, so he had knowledge that no other god possessed.

Odin was married to Frigg, the goddess of love and of the home, but he courted other goddesses and even giantesses. He had many children. When he was at Asgard, Odin held court at Valhalla, surrounded by warriors. In his hand he always held his spear Gungner, with which he could hurl down thunderbolts. Each day, two black ravens called Hugin and Mugin (Thought and Memory) flew silently over the earth. At dusk, the birds returned to perch on Odin's shoulders and give him a faithful account of all that was going on in the world below. When they saw a raven, the Vikings thought that they had perhaps come to the notice of one of Odin's messengers.

While Odin liked to spend time in reflection and meditation, he also loved to visit earth. He could soon reach any part of the world on his fabulous stallion Sleipnir. Sometimes he went in disguise, or even changed his shape so that he could mingle more easily among people. Strangely, Odin, for all his wisdom, was sometimes accompanied by evil and cunning Loki, and even took his advice.

Odin (right) was accompanied by two wolves and thirteen warrior maidens. Disguised as swans during times of peace, the Valkyries (left) rode to battle in human form.

THE IMMORTAL ASH TREE

The Vikings believed that the worlds were centred on a giant ash tree named Yggdrasil. Its roots grew down into an underground world, peopled by hostile forces. Around its trunk lay Midgard, the world in which humans lived, and in its highest branches, which touched the sun and the moon, was Asgard, the home of the gods.

The underground world

The three main roots of Yggdrasil plunged deep into the heart of the universe. The first reached a sacred spring, guarded by the three Norns. These were goddesses who un-ceasingly spun the threads of fate; when one of their threads broke, the life of a person ceased. Every day Urd, the eldest of the Norns, drew water from a magic fountain near which lived a pair of swans. All that came into contact with this water immediately turned white.

The second root led to the land of the dangerous frost giants. Not far from there sprang the fountain of wisdom, guarded by the giant Mimir, a friend of Odin.

The third root lead to Niflheim, 'land of mists', the world of the dead over which ruled the goddess Hel. Half of her face was as dark as the shadows surrounding her, while the other half was blue.

The eagle and the snake

The enormous trunk of Yggdrasil soared up through the centre of a world surrounded by tumultuous seas. Sometimes Odin tethered his stallion Sleipnir to the trunk of Yggdrasil; this was the only tree strong enough to hold his fiery steed, which could gallop faster than the wind.

In the branches lived strange animals, among them a little squirrel, Ratatosk, who cheerfully carried messages between the gods and the lower worlds.

At the very tip of Yggdrasil perched a golden cockerel, watching for any attack on Asgard. He was helped

by a white hawk who daily flew around the world to see that all was well.

Around the roots of Yggdrasil coiled an enormous snake, which gnawed away at them and caused earthquakes. Every day an eagle, a friend of the gods, swooped down from the highest branches to harass this monster. Happily, Yggdrasil was immortal, and was able to re-grow the damaged roots.

RAN AND HER DAUGHTERS

One day Ran the Robber, goddess of storms, was lurking by the Black Reef off the coast of Iceland. She loved to lie hidden in the frozen spray, a vast net in her hand with which she drew drowned sailors down to her home at the bottom of the sea.

At last a ship appeared: Erik and his companions were returning from the frozen shores of Greenland, worn out by a week of storms. Erik steered like a master through the dim early morning light. This was not the first time that he had made his way through frozen seas, and he knew how dangerous they could be. His father, Harald Redbeard, had taught him how to sail when he was only a little boy; he knew how to interpret the flight of the birds, the changing colours of the water and of the sky, and a thousand other signs which allowed him to escape most dangers. Above all, his father had warned him against Ran and her nine daughters.

Just as Erik was thinking of her, Ran sent a huge wave to sweep his boat on to the reef.

With a fearful crash the hull smashed against the rocks, and water poured in. Erik quickly sent some of his crew to push their ship off the rocks, and others to repair the breach; then, rowing with all their strength, they drew their ship clear of the reef.

Furious at their escape, Ran changed her tactics. Her nine daughters surrounded the boat, singing and dancing. Erik called to his men not to listen or look at them lest, fascinated by their beauty, they were dragged to the bottom of the sea. With eyes tight shut, and singing as loud as the goddesses, they drew on their oars and made their escape.

Ran and her daughters plunged in a rage to the great underwater palace of her husband, the

Ran the Robber, goddess of storms, lived deep at the bottom of the ocean with her husband Aegir and their nine daughters.

giant Aegir. He was deep in conversation with Njord, god of the sea. Njord was complaining about his wife Skadi. He told Aegir that Skadi did not like the ocean – which was difficult for the wife of the sea god. Their quarrel had lasted for many years: Skadi said that she was unable to sleep on Njord's boat because of the cries of the seagulls. Njord rejoined that he detested dry land, and he hated the howls of the great white wolves that roamed through the mountains where his wife would like to live. So the two had reached a compromise: for part of the year Njord lived at sea, with his friends and his gulls, while Skadi enjoyed her frozen wastes alone.

▷ THE SERPENT OF MIDGARD ◁

Erik and his crew, happy to have escaped Ran the storm goddess, regained the open sea. Although the waves were still strong, a pale glimmer of sunshine pierced the clouds. It cheered them up and made it easier for them to navigate.

A few days later, they reached the shores of a deserted island where they could have a brief rest. In a creek sheltered by high cliffs they scraped clean the hull, ate seal meat and, best of all, warmed themselves around a glowing fire of driftwood. There, as they drained their last barrels of beer, they planned their voyage home. A serious obstacle stood in their way to which no one dared openly refer; would they encounter the serpent of Midgard, whose body, coiled at the bottom of the oceans, was long enough to encircle the world?

Erik and his men set off on a fine morning with a fair wind. After several hours at sea, a short spurt of spray showed on the horizon. Then it disappeared and the sea was calm again. 'That must have been an illusion,' muttered Erik. But a few minutes later they saw the spray again. They rowed on in uneasy silence; the serpent must be there beneath the green waters, hidden among the rocks. Suddenly a powerful swell blotted out the horizon; it was the serpent of Midgard emerging, in a rage. Escape seemed impossible!

Erik was just wondering whether to change course when a vast wall of water and scales rose up in front of the ship. Too late now to think of a plan! Erik called to his crew to keep to their course, though death seemed certain. The ship was tossed into the air like a blown leaf, then crashed heavily back into the water – landing, by an amazing chance, on the other side of the serpent's body. The Vikings rowed for their lives to escape the surging waves around them.

Luckily the god Njord, who was fond of them, saw their difficulties. He sent favourable winds to help them to land. At last they reached their own village, nestling at the end of a fjord. That evening, everyone joined in a great feast.

Erik and his crew saw the scaly coils of the serpent of Midgard rise up before their ship.

14

THE CAPTURE OF FENRIR

Twice before the great wolf Fenrir had broken his bonds, simply by stretching and snapping the heavy iron chains as if they were fragile cords.

'How can we tie up such a powerful monster?' the gods asked themselves. They had to find an answer – and find it quickly, for an oracle had warned them that Fenrir was preparing to attack them. So they went to see the dwarfs. They asked these master smiths to make a bond so strong that no giant could ever break it.

'Give us time to think about this,' said the dwarfs. In great secrecy, they set to work. At last they brought the gods a long, silky ribbon which looked more like a lady's sash than a bond for the great wolf.

The gods thought that the dwarfs were joking, but the dwarfs challenged them to tear the ribbon. The first to try was Odin; he could not break it. Then Thor took his turn – with no more success. Next they tried together, one at each end. Tyr struck it two blows, first with his sword and then with an axe. All was in vain.

'This is amazing! What is the ribbon made from?' asked Odin.

The oldest dwarf reluctantly gave away part of the secret. 'We made it from a bear's tendons, a bird's saliva, the roots of a mountain, the mew of a cat, the beard of a woman and a fish's breath!' he said.

Now the gods had to persuade Fenrir to be tied up in the magic ribbon. They made it a friendly challenge, but their earlier efforts to trap him made him suspicious. The ribbon seemed innocent enough, but he insisted that one of the gods should keep a hand in his jaw during the test.

The gods were taken aback; who would dare take such a risk? But Tyr left the group and, without a word, placed his hand between the monster's teeth.

Soon the gods had tied up Fenrir. Then the great wolf strained to break loose – but to no avail. He was imprisoned by a flimsy ribbon! The gods congratulated themselves but Tyr remained solemn – and with good reason. The furious wolf, realizing that he was not going to be able to break free, bit off the god's hand.

Tyr turned pale with the pain. A goddess applied a magic ointment to heal his wound but Tyr, the god of courage and justice, remained one-handed for the rest of his days, for having kept his word without flinching.

Chains had failed to bind the great wolf Fenrir, but a flimsy ribbon held him fast.

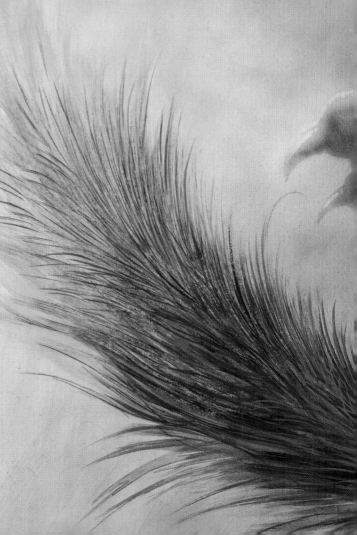

THE RING OF ANDVARI

Loki, the spirit of fire, was not one of the true gods, though he spent a lot of time with them. He often gave advice to Odin (and not always good advice), and he pretended to be a great friend of Thor, on whom he played some malicious tricks. In fact, Loki played a double game; he seemed to be the friend of the gods but he really wished to destroy their kingdom. To this end, he sowed discord among them as often as he could; and since he was clever and unscrupulous, he did this very well!

Loki owned magic shoes which allowed him to travel all over the world. He often spent time with the giants, to whom he was related, and he also visited the dwarfs. One day when he was sitting with Odin by a waterfall, Loki threw a stone at an otter and killed it. But this was no ordinary otter – it was a dwarf in disguise. Loki's victim was the son of a powerful magician, and his brothers were metalworking dwarfs. Enraged, they seized Odin's spear and Loki's magic shoes, and asked for a large amount of gold before they would give them back. Odin, who was annoyed by the whole business, sent Loki to the country of the black elves to find the ransom.

Loki was hungry when he reached this far country, and caught a large salmon with rainbow-coloured scales. It proved to be no salmon, but the dwarf Andvari who had changed his shape to enjoy a swim in the river. Andvari was a metalworker, and Loki realized his luck; he demanded all the gold the dwarf possessed as the price of his release. Andvari sullenly led Loki to his home and spread all his gold before him. All – or nearly all; for he hid away a magic gold ring. But Loki saw what he did and snatched the ring away. The angry dwarf cursed the ring, declaring that it would bring bad luck to anyone who owned it.

Loki gave a sour smile and went back to Odin, who was waiting impatiently for him. He was not disturbed by the curse, for he was not going to keep the ring himself! He poured out the ransom, including the gold ring. Loki and Odin took back their shoes and spear and went off together.

The magician's family soon quarrelled over the treasure. At last Fafnir, one of the brothers, carried it off to a barren and windswept country. Then he changed into a dragon and guarded his treasure by day and night.

'That ring is cursed!' cried the dwarf Andvari, as Loki carried off his most precious possession.

▷ SIGURD AND BRYNHILD ◁

The Valkyries were terrifying in battle, but in peacetime they changed into gentle swans. One day the Valkyries took off their swans' plumage to bathe, and this was stolen by a passing king. Without their wings the Valkyries became mere slaves, and the king made them fight for him. Odin was furious when this king began to win battles; and even more angry when he knew the role played by the Valkyries.

Odin blamed the most beautiful of the Valkyries, Brynhild. He struck her with his spear, and she fell into a trance. Around her Odin set a ring of fire.

One day, Sigmund and his warriors were gathered in their great hall, in the centre of which stood a tree. Suddenly a stranger entered the room. He was wrapped in a swirling cloak and a broad-brimmed hat hid his face; in his hand was a shining sword. An uneasy silence

fell. The stranger stepped forward a few paces, then plunged the sword up to its hilt in the tree trunk. 'This weapon will belong to he who can withdraw it,' he cried, and disappeared.

One by one the warriors heaved vainly at the sword. Then Sigmund strode up and drew it out. From then on he became invincible. Some years later, the stranger with the great hat and cape reappeared and challenged Sigmund to a duel. At the first blow his sword broke on the stranger's spear, from which came a flash of lightning. As Sigmund lay dying, he realized his opponent was Odin himself.

A few months later a child was born in a far-off land. He was brought up by a dwarf, and his name was Sigurd. One day the dwarf told Sigurd that he was Sigmund's son, gave him his father's sword which he had mended, and sent him to slay the dragon Fafnir.

Sigurd killed the dragon and seized And-vari's gold. As he rode on with the treasure, Sigurd came to the foot of a mountain encircled by fire. He drove his reluctant horse through the flames, and when they emerged he saw, to his astonishment, a beautiful sleeping girl. He leaned over and kissed her; she trembled, drew breath, and opened her eyes.

Sigurd and Brynhild fell deeply in love, but Sigurd owned the cursed ring, and they were tragically separated.

Sigurd's horse leapt bravely through the flames surrounding the beautiful Valkyrie Brynhild.

FOUR SHORT STORIES

THE SONS OF FENRIR

One morning young Bjorn was gazing uneasily at the sky. He had seen two immense clouds, shaped like wolves, which threatened to eclipse the sun and the moon. Bjorn, like all the Vikings, knew that this was a bad omen. Only the night before, he had heard that a litter of wolf cubs had been born to a giantess after the great wolf Fenrir had been captured by the gods. Now fully grown, these daring and ferocious sons of Fenrir ran through the skies chasing the stars.

At one moment Bjorn thought the wolf-cloud would swallow the sun completely. He was very frightened, for without the sun, the earth would be covered with snow in an everlasting winter.

Happily, towards midday, the sun quickened on its course. It drew away from the great black wolf, and shone as brilliantly as ever. Bjorn, reassured, continued on his way.

THE CAULDRON OF AEGIR

Aegir's underwater palace could not be lit by flames, but gold taken from the wrecks of Viking ships provided a brilliant light. Among Aegir's treasures was a magic cauldron, in which he made a marvellous brew destined for the gods. This was a mixture of beer and hydromel, and those who drank it quickly became calm and fell into a gentle sleep.

The gods loved to visit Aegir, who always gave them a warm welcome. Thor and Odin often joined these gatherings, when everyone sang and told stories before falling into a deep sleep.

22

Two giant wolves, sons of the monster Fenrir, race through the sky, threatening to swallow up the sun and the moon.

NJORD'S FEET

After the death of her father in a fight against the gods, the giantess Skadi took up his helmet and his weapons to avenge him. She strode to the home of the gods but, before a new war could break out, the gods suggested that to make up for her loss she could choose a husband from among them. However, in making her choice, all she was allowed to see of them was their feet. The gods hid behind a curtain, with only their feet visible. Skadi picked out the god with the most beautiful feet, dreaming (like so many women) that she would marry the kind and beautiful Balder.

Imagine her horror to find that she had picked out the elderly Njord, the god of the sea. Skadi and Njord were married all the same, but they spent the rest of their lives squabbling.

CHAMPION EATERS

On a journey to the land of the fire giants, Loki and Thor lodged with a magician. During their stay, Loki decided to issue a challenge, claiming that he had the largest appetite of anyone on earth.

The magician brought a giant called Logi to confront Loki. An enormous dish piled high with food was set before them, and they began to eat. At first the giant ate more slowly than Loki, then he ate more and more, faster and faster, even devouring the bones and the dish. Loki had lost, for he had forgotten that Logi personified fire – and the more its flames are fed, they more they can consume.

THOR AND THE SERPENT OF MIDGARD

From his earliest youth, Thor loathed all monsters, and in particular the enormous serpent of Midgard which lay at the bottom of the ocean. The body of this giant reptile encircled the earth, and its scaly coils caused many wrecks. It was seen only rarely, but its smallest movements in the ocean depths caused terrible storms.

When he was still a youth, Thor resolved to destroy the serpent. He set out to a distant region where lived a race of giant fishermen, who knew the serpent's habits. After much talk,

a giant called Hymir agreed to take Thor on his boat. Thor asked what sort of bait he would need. When Hymir would not answer him, Thor said no more: he took an ox belonging to the giant, cut off its head, and carried this on board the boat. Hymir doubted that the young god would be able to defeat the serpent, but he nevertheless pointed out to him an area where the serpent of the deep liked to lurk. Thor drew easily on his oars

24

until they reached the spot. Then he buried an enormous metal hook in the ox head, and fixed a strong rope to it. He threw it into the sea and waited as patiently as any ordinary fisherman.

Suddenly the rope stretched taut and the sea boiled around the boat, which bobbed up and down like a cork. Thor braced himself so firmly on the boat's hull that his feet broke through the timbers and he stood on the seabed. At last a fearsome head emerged from the water. Although Thor had hardly drawn on his full strength, his power was so immense that the serpent, hooked through its tongue, realized its danger. It coiled its body around the rocks far below the surface, and pulled as hard as it could.

Still Thor held the serpent's head above the water. Little by little the monster grew weaker, but still it spat venom and its bloodshot eyes flashed terrifyingly. It was so frightening that Hymir, crouched with chattering teeth in the bottom of the boat, panicked. He seized an axe and with one blow cut through the rope. Thor fell back, and in despair saw the serpent

disappear so fast that he had no chance to throw his hammer at it.

Thor flew into a terrible rage and decided to punish the wretch who had taken away his victory at the last moment. He knocked down the giant who had flouted him, and then abandoned him in his sinking boat.

For some time afterwards, the great serpent lay hidden deep in the ocean, licking its wounds. Unfortunately for the Vikings, it recovered and was able to haunt the seas again. They believed that it was the cause of many wrecks.

Young Thor seemed certain to catch the serpent of Midgard . . .

▷ THOR'S CHARIOT ◁

A storm was blowing up. The trembling of the ash leaves, the heavy air, and the low rumbling were all signs familiar to the Viking Harald. So he called to his young son: 'Bjorn! Thor is coming. I can hear him. Bring the animals quickly to shelter.'

The rumblings of Thor's chariot, drawn by two giant goats galloping across the sky, grew louder each minute. The god of thunder, son of Odin and the earth, was in a vile temper. Along his path a terrible storm broke out. Bjorn had just time to take shelter in the stable with the horses, where they pressed trembling one against the other, hoping that the god would not stop in their neighbourhood.

Thor was a gigantic god with a huge red beard. From time to time he fought with giants or monsters, but rarely with people, and he often gave his protection to women and children. Bjorn knew this, but his father had also told him that the god of thunder could be dangerous without meaning to be. His thunderous voice and enormous laugh had paralysed more than one person.

Most of the Vikings believed that Thor had no vices. He was married to the golden-haired goddess Sif, but he still fell in love with other goddesses, including the beautiful Freya. He also loved eating and drinking and, like his father Odin, he loved a good fight. Then he would take up his huge hammer which, like a boomerang, returned to its master's hand after he had hurled it at an enemy.

Thor lived in a many-roomed palace in Asgard, but he often travelled around the world, visiting people and other gods. He liked to disguise himself so that he was not recognized. Good natured and open hearted, he was not wary enough of the cunning Loki. One summer night, Loki stole up to the sleeping Sif and cut off her glorious golden hair. When Thor was woken next morning by her cries and tears he soon realised what had happened. He shook Loki until he promised to make up for his theft.

It was impossible to make Sif's hair grow again immediately, so Loki went to the dwarf smiths, and persuaded them to make a wonderful wig of purest gold. When he took it to Sif the next morning, her tears dried immediately. She loved it, but it made the other goddesses very jealous.

Bjorn feared the wrath of Thor the thunder god.

THOR AND THE GIANT KING

One evening, when Thor and his friends were fast asleep after a sumptuous banquet, someone slunk into the hall, quietly picked up Thor's hammer, and crept away again.

When Thor discovered the theft next morning, he flew into a terrible rage. To calm him down, someone suggested that Loki should find the thief. Loki realized that the hammer had probably been stolen by Thrym, the king of a tribe of giants. He borrowed the goddess Freya's magic cloak of feathers, and flew over the forest until he saw the giant seated on a hill.

Thrym admitted that he had stolen the magic hammer. 'I will only give it back if I can have Freya for my wife,' he said.

Loki was quite taken aback, for Freya, the goddess of love, was coveted by the most powerful gods and admired by all men for her beauty. As he had foreseen, she was furious when he told her of the giant's demand, and refused absolutely to live with such a great hulk as Thrym.

Thor threatened to destroy the giant's country, but Loki calmed him down. He reminded Thor that, without his hammer, he might well come to harm from his adversary. Thor saw his point. Loki persuaded the god to disguise himself as a woman and take Freya's place at the meeting arranged by the giants. Reluctantly Thor lent himself to the masquerade, and took the form of a young bride with a veil, diadem and Freya's fabulous gold necklace.

Thor harnessed his sacred goats and, guided by Loki, set out for the kingdom of the giants. After a long journey, he presented himself before Thrym and his brutish companions. They offered him something to eat as a sign of welcome. The hungry Thor, forgetting his disguise, ate his usual enormous meal – a whole ox, eight salmon, and all the desserts, washed down with three barrels of hydromel.

Thrym was astonished. 'I've never seen a young woman with such a terrific appetite,' he grumbled doubtfully.

Thor, recovering his wits, replied in a high voice, 'Freya has neither eaten nor drunk for eight days in her eagerness to see Thrym's palace.'

The flattered giant leaned forward to embrace his fiancée, but recoiled from the lightning flash of 'her' eyes. Before any such familiarity, said his bride, presents must be exchanged. The eager giant agreed and produced the magic hammer. Quick as a flash, Thor threw back his veil, seized the weapon, knocked out the giants and demolished their palace.

Thor, disguised as a young girl, presented himself before the giant Thrym.

THOR AND THE MAGICIAN

One dark moonless night, Thor and Loki took shelter in a strange cave, from which led five passages. Their sleep was disturbed by strange rumbling noises, and next morning they found the entrance blocked by a wall of leather. By using all his strength Thor managed to force a way through. He discovered that this wall was in fact one of the coat tails of a giant. The sounds which had broken their sleep were his snores. Then Thor looked at their 'cave' and understood: they had sheltered in a glove that the giant had thrown down. Thor picked up his hammer and tapped the giant on the head. He sat up with a groan, and led Thor and Loki to a strange castle and into a great hall crowded with giants.

Immediately the giant chief launched a series of challenges at Thor. First he had to empty in one draught a great vessel of beer. Thor gulped down the equivalent of several barrels, but the level of the beer fell hardly at all. Then, Thor had to pick up a black cat; this seemed easy, but he could not even lift its paws from the ground. Finally, the giant told him to wrestle with an old woman so frail that at first Thor hardly dared touch her; but try as he might, he was unable to push her over.

'What is this witchcraft?' cried Thor.

The chief admitted that he was a magician. 'The vessel of beer is connected to the ocean,' he explained. 'You could never empty that. The cat is an incarnation of the serpent of Midgard; it cannot be lifted up, for it is coiled around the world.'

'And the little old woman?'

'Ah, she is age itself – and no one can conquer age!'

Thor threw his hammer at the head of the giant, but before it reached its target, the magician and the castle disappeared.

Thor and Loki had spent the night in the giant's glove.

THE GUARDIAN OF THE RAINBOW

The home of the gods was connected to the world of men by a rainbow called Bifrost. At the top of the rainbow the god Heimdall stood guard day and night against a surprise attack from giants or monsters. A famous warrior, he had a magic sword called Hofur, made for him by the dwarfs, and a magic horn called Gjallarhorn, the sound of which could carry round the whole world.

Loki, who was always mulling over plans for the destruction of Asgard, hated Heimdall and regarded him as his principal enemy. He could not attack such a great warrior openly, but he played malicious tricks on him whenever he could. Above all, he tried to lure him away from Bifrost. Loki pretended to be Heimdall's friend, and often said what a shame it was that so great a warrior had to waste his time guarding an entrance.

'While you spend day after day at your post, soaked by the driving rain, the others are amusing themselves hunting, singing and drinking,' Loki would say, hoping to turn Heimdall against his friends. But the god knew how important his position was, and never listened. Sometimes he chased Loki away, but he always came back a few days later. Luckily, a golden cockerel also guarded Asgard, and he and Heimdall became firm friends. They kept each other company, for their worst enemy was boredom.

One day Loki stole the goddess Freya's fabulous golden necklace. Then he changed himself into a great white seal and ran off to hide his treasure on a far rock at the end of the western ocean.

Loki had forgotten Heimdall; from the top of his rainbow, he could see all over the world. Nothing escaped his eagle eye, and he had been watching Loki, whom he particularly distrusted. He vaulted on to his horse Gulltopr, and in one great leap arrived on the far shore. There he changed himself into another seal and chased Loki though the grey waters and iceflows to the end of the world. Loki plunged to the deepest abysses to shake off his adversary, but Heimdall always found his track. In the end the two seals came face to face on a wave-battered reef. Heimdall thrashed Loki soundly, and he crept off to plot his revenge.

The god took the necklace back to shore, where he changed back to his usual form. With the speed of lightning, he crossed the rainbow on his horse and entered Asgard. All the gods thanked him and wished to organize a great feast, but Heimdall would not stay. He just handed over the necklace to Freya, and took up his post again.

Loki, for all his cunning, could not distract Heimdall as he stood watch over Asgard.

▷ THE DEATH OF BALDER ◁

Balder the sun god was loved by everyone for his goodness and gentleness. But one night he dreamed his life was threatened.

When he told his mother, the goddess Frigg, she was very worried. To safeguard her son, she asked everything on earth to swear not to hurt him. So Balder became invulnerable. The gods enjoyed throwing things at him, laughing when their missiles glanced off him without so much as scratching him.

Evil Loki felt sure Balder must have a weak point. He disguised himself as an old woman and went to see Frigg, who explained why her son was never wounded. 'Everything has sworn never to hurt him,' she said.

'Everything?' asked Loki insistently.

'Yes,' replied Frigg, but after a short pause she added that she had forgotten a sprig of mistletoe. Loki raced off, found the mistletoe, and cut it.

Now Loki thought up a hateful plan. He went to Balder's blind brother Hoder.

'Why do you never join in throwing things at Balder?' asked the evil spirit.

'Because I am blind!' smiled the god.

'If you like, I will guide your hand as you throw,' offered Loki. So he made a weapon from the mistletoe bough, and directed the blind god's hand. The arrow flew straight at Balder, who fell dead.

The gods were devastated, and Balder's brother Hermod went to plead with Hel, goddess of the underworld, who said that if every single living thing called for his return, Balder could go back to Asgard.

Such agreement was easily gained, but as Hermod travelled back to the underworld he met an old sorcerer who refused to say yes. It was Loki in disguise. Because of his opposition, Balder remained Hel's prisoner.

When the gods discovered Loki's schemes they chained him in a cave full of snakes.

Loki tricked the blind god to release the arrow that struck Balder.

THE TWILIGHT OF THE GODS

After the death of Balder, many signs warned the gods that their world was threatened. Stars fell from the sky, the land quaked and groaned and even Yggdrasil was shaken. Beneath the ground the dog of Hell howled night and day. A violent tempest uprooted trees and cast ships on the rocks. The two great wolf-clouds swallowed up the sun and the moon. The cock Golden-kammer sounded the alarm and Heimdall blew his trumpet with all his strength.

Silently the gods lined up around Asgard, determined to defend it to the end. They were faced by a strange gathering of giants and monsters, led by Loki and the great wolf Fenrir, who had escaped their bonds.

Odin, surrounded by his Valkyries, was first to throw himself into the battle. But Fenrir had marked him down and snapped him up, as an oracle had foretold. Vidar, one of Odin's sons, struck down Fenrir. Thor at last killed the serpent of Midgard, only to die poisoned by its breath. Tyr felled the dog of Hell before falling in his turn. Loki led a troop of giants up the rainbow Bifrost and they flung themselves at Heimdall. He killed them all but died from his wounds. Finally the fire giants set all Asgard alight.

At last both sides had destroyed each other. This was Ragnarok, the end of the first world.

In vain the gods defended their world.

▷ THE NEW WORLD ◁

After the catastrophe of Ragnarok, the sky was hidden by black ashes and thick clouds of smoke. The land was submerged by tumultuous seas. People, gods, giants and monsters had all disappeared.

At last a new sun and a new moon arose again. Little by little, their light warmed the world once more. The clouds of smoke blew away and the flood waters subsided.

Although most of the gods, the giants and the monsters had perished, some were able to return to earth. Odin and Thor were gone for ever, but some of their sons reappeared. The first to escape from Hell was Balder. He was determined to make the new world better than the first. He was joined by Forseti, god of justice, and his brothers Hoder the blind, Vali, Vidar (who fought so bravely to kill Fenrir) and Hermod, who risked his life to plead for Balder's return from the underworld. With Thor's sons Magni and Modi, they formed a council of gods to oversee the organization of the new world. They were helped by the old gods' rune-carved stones which they learned to read.

At first, there were no people on earth. But fortunately, the gods found a man and a woman who had survived the catastrophe, protected by the bark of Yggdrasil, the giant ash tree which ran through the centre of the world. The gods released this couple immediately and they soon peopled the world with their many children. Plants and animals also reappeared.

Under the watchful eyes of the council of the gods, order came to the world again. Even dwarfs reappeared in the depths of the forests, and elves danced in the moonlight.

Although all the monsters seemed to have disappeared, some giants could have taken refuge in the farthest regions of ice and fire. Some Vikings thought they saw the coils of a vast serpent at the bottom of the sea. Could they have been dreaming?

The sons of the gods watched over the building of a new, wiser world.

Bjorn watched the elves, longing to join them.

CREATURES OF THE NIGHT

Young Bjorn could not get to sleep. The night before he had seen a lovely young girl in the forest; she had smiled at him, then disappeared. He quietly opened the door and stole out, although his father Harald had told him how dangerous it was to be in the forest on moonlit nights.

Bjorn went deeper and deeper into the forest. Suddenly, he was startled by the noise of snapping twigs and a bright light appeared through the mist. A great luminous mass rushed past him; it was the sacred golden boar of the god Frey, and to see it was a good omen!

Before long Bjorn was deeper in the forest than ever before. Soon he thought that he could hear singing. He came to a clearing bathed in moonlight and to his astonishment saw a group of dancing elves, twisting and turning with lightning speed. Among them was the lovely girl he had seen the day before. The Vikings often spoke of the elves but very seldom saw them – which was lucky, for the elves might carry them off for ever.

Bjorn hesitated to join them for he knew how dangerous this might be. But the temptation was too great; he leapt from his hiding place and held out his hand. But just as shining fingers took his hand, a cock crowed. Night had ended, and immediately the elves disappeared. Bjorn was saved.

Alone in the clearing, the boy thought he must have been dreaming. But no: as the light of dawn touched the dew on the grass, he could see the faint traces of the elves' flying feet.

The Kobolds worked unseen to help the deserving poor.

▷ THE KOBOLDS ◁

One cold autumn morning Snorre went into the barn, a heavy bucket of fresh water in each hand. To his astonishment a sturdy little man was grooming the old horse while another gave hay to the pony. A third mucked out the animals, while a fourth repaired a cask. When they saw Snorre, they ran away!

Snorre had seen the Kobolds, who lived in the barns and stables of deserving people. As they worked at night, they were seldom seen. Snorre and his sister Asfrid had struggled to keep the farm running and feed the family while their father was away. The next night they hid until the Kobolds appeared; then they thanked the little people for all their help.

▷ THE FOREST DWARFS ◁

The following spring Snorre and Asfrid's little sister fell seriously ill. They went into the woods to search for herbs to cure her, but although they looked for a long time they could find none. As they turned sadly home a muffled noise in the branches of a nearby thicket drew their attention. They peered between its twigs and saw a group of dwarfs – not the Kobolds this time, but the dwarfs of the forest. These rough little people, dressed in animal skins, knew where every plant grew and where every animal hid.

The oldest dwarf came towards Snorre and Asfrid, and asked them what they were doing so far from home. When the children explained, the dwarfs felt sorry for them. They vanished, only to reappear a few seconds later with a huge bunch of healing herbs. Snorre and Asfrid thanked them, and then ran home as fast as they could. Soon their sister was cured, with the help of the herbs.

Each spring, for years afterwards, Snorre and Asfrid made their way to a clearing deep in the forest. There they met the forest dwarfs, who had become their friends.

The forest dwarfs were also kind to humans.

FROM LEGEND TO HISTORY

The Vikings came from Scandinavia. At home they were farmers and fishermen. But they were also great sailors, and from the 8th century on, as their homelands became overcrowded, they spread across the northern world to settle in the Faroes, the British Isles, Iceland and Greenland, and even briefly on the coasts of North America.

The Vikings journeyed across the stormy northern seas in sturdy ships, propelled by oars and sails. Their ships were able to navigate shallow waters, and Viking traders travelled down the rivers of Russia, setting up trading posts. Some of their merchants reached Constantinople and even Baghdad. They exchanged furs, amber, walrus ivory, dried fish and timber for silks, spices and silver.

But the Vikings were also fierce warriors. Records tell of their terrifying raids on wealthy monasteries and towns, from which they carried off all the valuable objects they could. In time, raiders began to settle in the areas they had invaded. In the mid 9th century Vikings from Denmark began to settle in eastern England, and in 878 a treaty was signed giving them control over a large area known as the Danelaw. They had a flourishing settlement at York; we know about it from Viking remains found there, and from the Anglo-Saxon Chronicle, a record kept by monks which tells of Viking kings ruling in York in the early 10th century. Many place names in eastern England, such as those including '-thorpe', have Viking origins.

In 911 a large area in northern France was handed over to the Vikings; it is called Normandy, the land of the men from the North, after them. The kings of England and France hoped that in return for ceding them territory the Viking raids would cease, but they still continued to some extent.

The Oséberg ship (below) dates from the 8th century. It was excavated as part of a Viking burial in Norway.

A warrior's helmet (right), part of the Vendel treasure in the Historical Museum, Stockholm.

Norway's coast (right) has many long, narrow inlets called fjords. The Viking people lived by the sea and were fearless sailors.

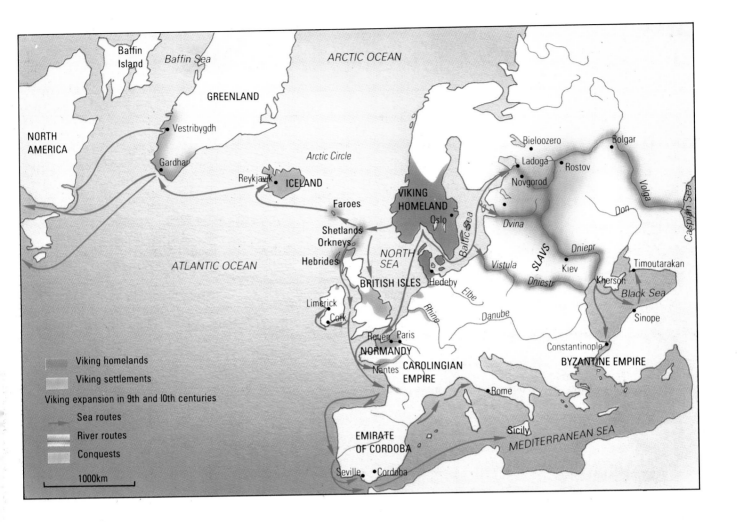

Gods of the sea

The Viking gods were crude and violent, reflecting the dreams of these conquering seafarers. They were anxious to keep themselves in favour with the many sea gods. Foremost was Njord, an old man who watched over the coastal shores and gave the fishermen their catch. Beneath the sea Aegir, his wife Ran the storm goddess and their nine daughters lived in a mysterious palace. The Vikings distinguished nine different types of wave, and thought each was produced by one of Ran's daughters. These beautiful sirens lured sailors down to their underwater home. Violent storms were attributed to the serpent of Midgard, which curled itself right around the world beneath the waves.

These gods reflected both the riches and the dangers of the sea and its powerful attraction for men.

The rival gods

The Viking gods, like people, were very different from one another and often they quarrelled. They were divided into two great families, the Aesir and the Vanir. Odin, the chief god, was recognized by most of the Vikings, but he did not have complete authority over the other gods. Over the centuries Thor, the god of thunder became more and more popular, particularly with sailors and peasants, who more often prayed to him than to Odin.

As in many religions with numerous gods, the goddesses played an important part. Many little figures dedicated to Freya have been found, so she was probably one of the most important goddesses.

The Vikings did not find it confusing to worship a number of gods. They liked to think of a crowd of gods and goddesses, often squabbling among themselves, peopling the skies, oceans and rivers.

A religion without temples

The Vikings were sailors, not builders, and apart from a brief description of a temple at Uppsala in Sweden, there is no trace of a Viking temple or shrine. It seems that they felt no need for buildings in which to worship or make sacrifices. Usually large trees, in particular ashes, served as meeting places. Feasts, assemblies and probably sacrifices took place at the foot of such giant trees, and simple shrines may have been set up there.

The Vikings had no priests or religious leaders of any sort. In early days they did not even have kings, although such old men as the heads of families and famous warriors exerted a moral authority (and possibly a religious one too) over the other Vikings. A family would own a few little figures depicting gods, to which they offered sacrifices, each praying in their own way, for there were no set patterns and the Viking religion varied from one region to another.

In the course of their journeys, the Vikings came increasingly into contact with other religions. In 966, Harald Bluetooth was baptised and from then on, little by little, all the Vikings became Christians.

The giants

The Vikings, like many other peoples, believed that the gods were not the first beings to appear on earth. Before them came giants and all sorts of monsters. The Vikings thought that the giants had not disappeared; conquered by the gods, they had withdrawn to far distant regions, living in the 'land of ice', the 'land of fire' and deep underground.

The giants were often rough, dangerous and violent, but some of them were clever, among them the builder of Asgard and Mimir, who guarded the fountain of wisdom. But most lived like animals, and made friends of monstrous beasts.

There were also several kinds of dwarfs. Metalworkers lived under the earth, where they forged weapons and magic jewels. No one could learn their secret skills. Other dwarfs, called Kobolds, sometimes lived around the houses of fortunate Vikings. At night they helped with the heaviest tasks, and the only evidence of their presence was that of the jobs they had carried out. People very rarely saw them, but they left out milk and scraps of food for them.

The dwarfs were friendly towards both gods and men, but usually avoided them. If they were harmed in any way, they became angry – hence the curse of the dwarf Andvari when Loki stole his ring.

The Vikings feared the elves, who were quite different from the dwarfs. They were beautiful young creatures who appeared on moonlit nights, dancing in a circle in clearings, and lured away adolescents. Anyone who joined their dance left the human world; when the first cock crowed at dawn, the elves disappeared. Fleeting and elusive, they symbolized the desires of youth, and were seldom seen by adults.

This carved stone from the Historical Museum of Stockholm shows (bottom right) the god Odin on his eight-legged stallion Sleipnir.

Mortal gods

The Vikings, unlike most peoples, believed that their gods were mortal – and always under threat. They grew old very slowly and it was not time that menaced them, but a combination of giants and monsters such as the wolf Fenrir and the serpent of Midgard. The gods also had false friends, such as Loki the troublemaker, who lived among them while plotting how best to attack Asgard.

The Vikings thought that two giant wolves chased the sun and moon each day. If ever they caught them and swallowed them up, the end of the world would be at hand, for men as well as for gods. In their legends the end of the world took the form of a series of natural catastrophies – including earthquakes, tempests and tidal waves – and above all an attack on Asgard. The final battle was called the Ragnarok in Scandinavia, and the Twilight of the Gods by the people of northern Germany. Today these stories are best known from the operas of Richard Wagner, in the German version.

So the world of the Vikings was destined to disappear in a final conflict, during which everyone must give proof of that most important virtue: courage.

From Iceland came stories of how the world might have been reborn. Some of the lesser gods reappeared and organized a new world. A man and a woman were found hidden beneath Yggdrasil's bark and their descendants repeopled the new world, which was peaceful and without demons. Some scholars think that they see Christian influence in this last episode: the old pagan world had disappeared and a new and better world had taken its place.

Vikings, Germans and Celts

The mythology of the Vikings disappeared gradually, like most of the pagan religions of northern Europe, around AD 1000. However, most of the old German legends of warlike gods, Valkyries, dwarfs and dragons had their roots in Viking myths. Some personages were simply transferred with changed names; Sigurd, for example, became Siegfried. Variations

as runes. It is possible to read them to some extent, since the meaning of each sign is known, but scholars can make different interpretations.

Many runic stones are found in Scandinavia. They are often decorated with interlacing patterns, and sometimes painted in bright colours.

We can learn more about the Viking civilization from the records of neighbouring peoples. However, for studying their mythology, the most valuable sources are the long Icelandic poems which were memorized and handed down from one generation to the next, until they were collected and written down in the Middle Ages. Epic stories also tell of the exploits of Icelandic sailors, in verse or in prose.

Much of our knowledge of the Vikings comes from their burial places, for they believed that the dead should be surrounded by objects they had used in life and which they would need in the next world. These include many household objects, weapons, and even ships and chariots. Religious objects include little figures of gods, amulets and pendants, a favourite being a miniature version of the hammer of the god Thor.

These stones, arranged in the form of a ship, mark a Viking burial at Vastmanland, Sweden.

appeared in the retelling, but the main thread remained the same. The stories of the cursed Rhinegold, for example, come directly from the stories of Sigurd and the cursed ring of Andvari. Some episodes were common to the Vikings, the Germans and the Celts, as for example the legend of a sword stuck fast in a rock (or a tree) which is found in the legends of the Round Table, and that of the magic hammer which belonged to both Thor and the Celtic god Taranis.

Mysterious writing

The Vikings wrote little. Those among them who mastered the art used straight letters designed to be carved on stone, bone or wood, rather than rounded letters to be written with a pen or brush. These strange letters are known

RUNES

Runes – angular letters usually found carved in stone or wood – were used by the Vikings and the first Germans. According to myth, they were invented by Odin, the wisest of the gods. They appeared around the year AD1000, and their origin is still uncertain.

This form of writing has often been thought mysterious. It is made up mostly of right-angled lines, which would have been easy to carve, and has no strict alphabet. The six first letters are f u th a r k, and the system is known as futhark. One form of futhark is made up of 24 signs, a second of only 16.

This stone is carved with runic letters and a stylised beast with characteristic interlacing decoration.

INDEX